NATURE DETECTIVE

British Butterflies

A Photographic Guide

Victoria Munson

WAYLAND

First published in 2017 by Wayland

Wayland
50 Victoria Embankment
London EC4Y 0DZ

Wayland Australia
Level 17/207 Kent Street
Sydney, NSW 2000

Designer: Elaine Wilkinson
Editor: Victoria Brooker
Consultant: Butterfly Conservation

A cataloguing record for this title is available
at the British Library.
ISBN: 978 1 5263 0 1574

Printed in China

MIX
Paper from
responsible sources
FSC® C104740
www.fsc.org

Wayland, part of Hachette Children's Group and
published by Hodder and Stoughton Limited.
www.hachette.co.uk

Acknowledgements:
FLPA: 46 (inset) Arik Siegel/Nature in Stock/
FLPA; 46 (main) Gianpiero Ferrari/FLPA; 36, 53
Neil Hulme, Butterfly Concervation Shutterstock.
com 2, 29 Chris2766; 2r, 3r 32, 33 (inset) aaltair;
3l, 41 Torsten Dietrich; 4t, 29, 30 (main) hfuchs;
5 Lyudmyla Kharlamova; 6t dedek; 6bl Nikiteev_
Konstantin; 6br Stanislaw Tokarski; 7t Brian
Lasenby; 7m Paul Broadbent; 7b Jausa; 8 Hannu
Rama; 9, 13, 15, 26, 27, 46, 50, 52 main and
inset MarkMirror; 10, 23, 32, 37, 40, 54 Martin
Fowler; 11, 31, 45, 62 alslutsky; 12 artconcept;
14 Myroslav Vydrak; 17 Peter Reijners; 17 inset
HHelene; 18 Mirvav; 19 AdamEdwards; 20
Stephen Farhall; 21 Pixeljoy; 22 Robert Trevis-
Smith; 24 (main) dmik; 24 (inset), 44, 63 Vitalii
Hulai; 25, 34 Emjay Smith; 27, 39, 48 (inset),
56 (main) Bildagentur Zoonar GmbH; 28 (main)
Viasta Kaspar; 28 (inset) Ivan Marjanovic; 30
(inset), 42 Sue Robinson; 33 (main), 43, 49 (main)
61, 64 Rudmer Zwerver; 35, 60B Carmen Rieb; 38
Marek R. Swadzba; 41 Andreas Eichler/ Wikimedia
Commons; 47 TTstudio; 48 (main) Florian
Andronache; 49 (inset), 54 (inset) jps; 51Kostyuk
Alexander; 55 (main) Roger Meerts; 55 (inset)
Vitaly Ilyasov; 56 (inset) Henrik Larsson; 57 (main)
pokku; 57(inset) Maria Jeffs; 58m Arjen Visser;
58b Jeanette Dietl; 60 Talslutsky; 59: Artwork by
Peter Bull

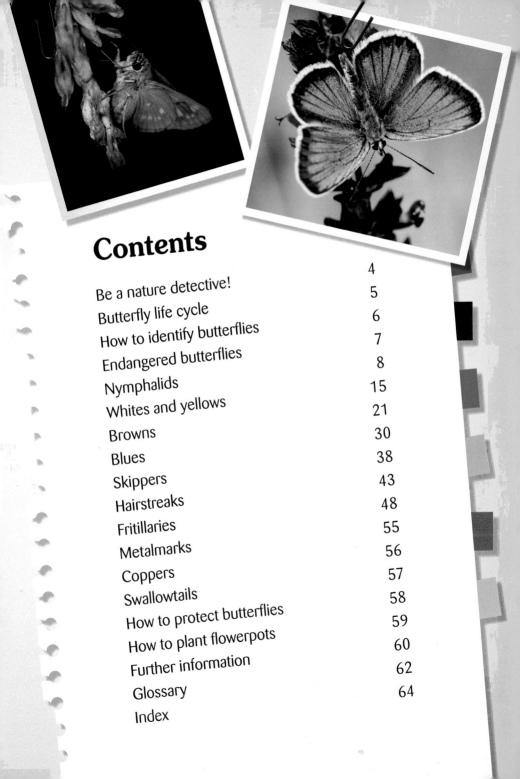

Contents

Be a nature detective!

To be a nature detective, you need to be observant. This means looking around you. Butterflies can be seen all year, but the best time to look for butterflies is in spring and summer.

What is a butterfly?

A butterfly is an insect. All insects have three parts to their bodies: a head, a thorax (middle) and an abdomen (lower part). On their head, they have a pair of antennae, which they use for smelling and feelings. Most insects have a pair of eyes and all insects have three pairs of jointed legs. Butterflies also have a proboscis, a hollow tube through which they suck up food, such as nectar.

antenna

eye

head

forewing

forewing

thorax

hindwing

hindwing

abdomen

Butterfly life cycle

Butterflies have four separate stages to their life cycle, changing from egg, to caterpillar, to chrysalis, to butterfly. This process is called metamorphosis. It begins when the female butterflies lay eggs on plants. Most of the time the female lays her eggs on or near a plant that her caterpillars like to eat. The eggs can be round or oval, smooth or wrinkly. In some species, they will hatch in a few weeks. In others, they won't hatch until the weather is warm enough.

When they are ready, the caterpillars leave their eggs and start to eat lots of leaves. As they get bigger, their skin splits and they shed it to reveal a new skin underneath. This happens four or five times.

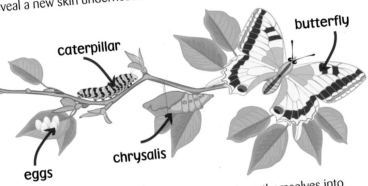

caterpillar

butterfly

chrysalis

eggs

When they are big enough, the caterpillars form themselves into a chrysalis. They usually do this on twigs or in bushy plants. Most chrysalises are green or brown, so that they are camouflaged and protected. Sometimes this stage takes a few weeks, sometimes a few months. Many stay as chrysalises through the winter and emerge as butterflies in spring.

When a butterfly is ready, the chrysalis splits. The butterfly is wet, so it must wait for its wings to dry before its first flight. Then it can flutter away to find flowers for nectar and also look for a mate, so that another life cycle can begin.

A fully grown caterpillar is at least 100 times larger than when it emerged from its egg.

How to identify butterflies

There are around 60 species of butterfly in the UK. Some of them look very similar. Take a notebook with you when you're out and about. When you spot a butterfly, make a quick sketch of it. Note down what colour it is, estimate its size and write where you saw it. You can then use this book to help you identify which butterfly it is.

Where to find butterflies

Butterflies live in almost every type of habitat in Britain, from coasts and mountains to moorland and woodland. Look for them on a day out or if you're on a school trip. Your chances of spotting butterflies are better on warm or sunny spring and summer days.

Saturday 12 June   meadow walk

white spots

orange

black spots all over

Endangered butterflies

Butterflies have been on Earth for at least 50 million years and may have first evolved 150 million years ago. They are an important part of British wildlife, helping to pollinate plants, so that plants can produce seeds and continue their life cycle. Butterflies, caterpillars and moths are also a vital link in food chains, as birds, bats and other animals eat them.

Many butterflies are endangered because their habitats are changing or are even disappearing altogether. Some butterflies and their caterpillars feed on only one or two types of plants. If there aren't enough of these plants around, then there will be fewer and fewer of that species of butterflies, until eventually, they will become extinct. Butterflies are very sensitive to changes in their environment, often needing a special set of conditions to complete their life cycle. Find out how you can help to protect butterflies on pages 58–59.

Peacock

Scientific name: *Aglais io*
Wingspan: 63-69 mm
Habitat: Most habitats
Family: Nymphalids

This common garden
butterfly has striking yellow and
blue eyespots on the tip of each wing.
These spots give the butterfly its name because
they look like the markings on a peacock bird. In winter,
Peacock butterflies hibernate in hollow trees and sheds.

Comma

Scientific name: *Polygonia c-album*
Wing span: 55–60 mm
Habitat: Woodland, gardens
Family: Nymphalids

Comma butterflies are easily recognised by their curved and
ragged wing edges. They are orange butterflies with black markings.
Their undersides are brown with a white, comma-shaped mark.
Commas like to rest head downwards on the bark of birch or ash
trees, or on leaves.

Painted Lady

Scientific name: *Vanessa cardui*
Wingspan: 58-74 mm
Habitat: Most habitats
Family: Nymphalids

Painted Ladies look similar to
Small Tortoiseshells, but Painted Ladies are
salmon-coloured and have a large patch of black
on the corner of each forewing that is dotted with white.
The caterpillars have a black body with yellow stripes along it.
Painted Lady butterflies start to come to Britain from Africa and
the Mediterranean in March, and then all through the summer.

Small Tortoiseshell

Scientific name: *Aglais urticae*
Wingspan: 45-62 mm
Habitat: Most habitats
Family: Nymphalids

Small Tortoiseshell
butterflies are bright orange
with black and yellow bars on their
forewings, and black arches filled with blue
edging on all four wings. Female Tortoiseshells
will lay between 80 and 100 eggs on the underside
of nettle leaves.

Red Admiral

Scientific name: *Vanessa atalanta*
Wingspan: 64-78 mm
Habitat: Most habitats
Family: Nymphalids

These striking red and black butterflies are common visitors to gardens and are easily recognisable. They have bars of red on their fore and hindwings, with white spots on the tips of their forewings. The underside of their wings is dark brown and black, which provides good camouflage when they rest on tree bark.

White Admiral

Scientific name: *Limenitis camilla*
Wingspan: 60–64 mm
Habitat: Woodlands
Family: Nymphalids

White Admiral butterflies like to feed off bramble

White Admirals have black upper wings with one long white stripe across each wing. The underwings are gingery brown. They have a distinctive flight of short wing beats followed by a long glide. White Admirals occur widely in southern England. Their caterpillars will only feed on honeysuckle plants.

13

Purple Emperor

Scientific name: *Apatura iris*
Wingspan: 75-84 mm
Habitat: Woodland
Family: Nymphalids

This large butterfly is hard to spot because it spends so much of its time feeding in treetops. Purple Emperors are also quite rare, found only in woodland in southern England. Males might be seen in the early mornings when they fly down to feed on salts from damp puddles, or on animal droppings. Males are glossy purple above, with white bands and orange-ringed eyespots. Females are larger, dark-grey brown and look like White Admirals.

Whites and yellows

Orange-tip

Scientific name: Anthocharis cardamines
Wingspan: 45-50 mm
Habitat: Riverbanks, hedgerows, meadows
Family: Whites and yellows

Orange-tip butterflies get their name from the males that have striking orange tips on their white forewings. Female forewings are white, but with black tips and one black spot. Females look very similar to Small Whites, but Orange-tip males and females have mottled undersides.

Brimstone

Scientific name: *Gonepteryx rhamni*
Wingspan: 60–74 mm
Habitat: Grassland, damp woodland, hedgerows
Family: Whites and yellows

Brimstones have noticeably pointed, leaf-shaped wings. Females have pale green wings with an orange spot in the middle. Males have more yellowy-green underwings than females and yellow upperwings. Brimstones have a very long proboscis that helps them to feed on nectar deep inside flowers.

Green-veined White

Scientific name: *Pieris napi*
Wingspan: 40-52 mm
Habitat: Woodland, meadows, hedgerows, riverbanks
Family: Whites and yellows

When Green-veined Whites wings are closed, you can clearly see greenish-grey veins on the underwings. They look like Small Whites when their wings are open. However, Green-veined Whites also prefer damp areas to the farmland and gardens where Small Whites are found. Green-veined Whites' forewings have a black tip. Males have a central black spot on the forewings and females have two spots.

Large White

Scientific name: *Pieris brassicae*
Wingspan: 63-70 mm
Habitat: Gardens, parks and farmland
Family: Whites and yellows

Large White butterflies look very
similar to Small Whites, but Large Whites are,
as the name gives away, slightly larger and their
black markings are much darker. Females have two black
spots and males have no spots. Caterpillars are grey-green
and mottled, with black spots and yellow stripes. They stay as
pupae through winter, and adults emerge in spring. The caterpillars
eat cabbages, so they are not popular with farmers or gardeners.

Small White

Scientific name: *Pieris rapae*
Wingspan: 38-57 mm
Habitat: Gardens, parks and farmland
Family: Whites and yellows

One of the most common butterflies in Britain, the Small White is, as its name suggests, small and white. The females have two black spots and a black streak on the forewings. Males also have two black spots, but the second of these spots is much lighter. Small White caterpillars are a pest for farmers, because they eat cabbages and Brussels sprouts.

Wood White

Scientific name: Leptidea sinapis
Wingspan: 42 mm
Habitat: Woodland
Family: Whites and yellows

The Wood White is a small, dainty butterfly. The upperwings are white with rounded edges. Males have a black mark on the edge of the forewing. The undersides are white with grey patches. In sunny weather, males are often seen fluttering gently around looking for females. Females spend most of their time feeding or resting on flowers.

Marbled White

Scientific name: *Melanargia galathea*
Wingspan: 53–58 mm
Habitat: Grassland, woodland
Family: Browns

Look for these butterflies between June and August.

This butterfly is unmistakable with its distinctive black-and-white, checked wings. Despite its name, the Marbled White is actually a member of the Brown family as it has the characteristic eyespots of this family.

Large Heath

Scientific name: *Coenonympha tullia*
Wingspan: 41 mm
Habitat: Bogs, moorland
Family: Browns

The Large Heath is usually seen with its wings closed, On its brown underwings there are six black eye spots and a white band. The size of the spots varies depending on where it is found in Britain.

Small Heath

Scientific name: *Coenonympha pamphilus*

Wingspan: 34–38 mm

Habitat: Grassland, woodland, coasts

Family: Browns

This small yellow–orange butterfly only flies in sunshine. It flies very close to the ground, at no more than 1 metre high. Most commonly seen with its wings closed, it has one prominent black eyespot on an orange underwing.

You can see Small Heaths from late April right through to September.

Ringlet

Scientific name: *Aphantopus hyperantus*
Wingspan: 48–52 mm
Habitat: Grassland, woodland
Family: Browns

Ringlets get their name from the small circles on their underwings.
These ringlets vary in number and size between butterflies. The rings
have a white centre, surrounded by a black ring and a yellow outer ring.
This velvet-looking butterfly can look almost black when young with a faint
white fringe around its upper wings. Ringlets fly with a bobbing movement.

24

Gatekeeper

Scientific name: *Pyronia tithonus*
Wingspan: 40-47 mm
Habitat: Hedgerows, grassland
Family: Browns

As its name suggests, this butterfly is often found in gateways or hedgerows. It has orange-brown wings, fringed with a grey-brown border, and black-and-white eyespots on each upper wing. The combination of one large eyespot on forewing and one small eyespot on hind wing is unique to Gatekeepers. Gatekeepers are often seen near Ringlets and Meadow Browns, but are easily identified because Gatekeepers often bask in the sunshine with open wings.

Meadow Brown

Scientific name: *Maniola jurtina*
Wingspan: 40-60 mm
Habitat: Grassland, meadows and woodland
Family: Browns

Meadow Browns are mainly brown with bright orange-brown patches on their forewings, in each of which is a black eyespot. These eyespots are used to scare away predators, such as birds. Female Meadow Browns are slightly brighter-coloured than males and have a larger eyespot. They are one of our commonest butterflies.

Scotch Argus

Scientific name: *Erebia aethiops*
Wingspan: 35-40 mm
Habitat: Grassland
Family: Browns

These dark, chocolate-brown butterflies have black-and-white eye spots set in orange patches. As their name suggests, they are found mostly in Scotland. In summer, males are very active, flying almost without rest. In contrast, the females spend a lot of time basking in the sun.

Wall

Scientific name: *Lasiommata megera*
Wingspan: 44-46 mm
Habitat: Grassland and coasts
Family: Browns

This butterfly gets its name because it can often be found basking on walls, stones and bare ground. It is very similar in size and colour to the Gatekeeper, but Wall butterflies are much more patterned. Their undersides are light and provide good camouflage against stony and sandy habitats. Wall butterflies have one large eyespot on the forewings and four smaller eyespots on the hindwings.

Speckled Wood

Scientific name: *Pararge aegeria*
Wingspan: 40-55 mm
Habitat: Woodland, gardens and hedgerows
Family: Browns

Speckled Wood butterflies like to perch in sunny spots.

Speckled Woods are mainly brown with creamy-yellow dots on their wings. They also have several eyespots; one on the tip of each forewing and three eyespots on each hindwing. Their undersides are a marbled light and dark brown. Females are larger than males and have slightly darker markings. Speckled Wood caterpillars are light yellowish-green with a dark-green stripe along the back and lines along the side.

Adonis Blue

Scientific name: *Polyommatus bellargus*
Wingspan: 30-40 mm
Habitat: Chalk and limestone grassland
Family: Blues

This striking butterfly is found mainly across the south of England. Males are bright sky-blue and females are brown. Both have a black outline around white patches at the edge of their wings. Underwings have black and orange spots. They like to fly low across the ground to feed on grasses.

Large Blue

Scientific name: *Maculinea arion*
Wingspan: 38-44 mm
Habitat: Limestone grassland
Family: Blues

The Large Blue is
Britain's largest, but also rarest,
blue butterfly. The Large Blue became
extinct in Britain in 1979, but has since been
reintroduced from Europe. It has black spots on its
blue upperwings and black spots on brown underwings.

Small Blue

Scientific name: *Cupido minimus*
Wingspan: 20-30 mm
Habitat: Grassland, coasts,
sand dunes, urban habitats
Family: Blues

With its wings open, this butterfly looks
brown with a pale blue dusting, but when its
wings are closed, you can see the very pale blue–grey
underwings that give it its name. Small Blue caterpillars only
feed on kidney vetch plants, which are becoming rarer and,
therefore, Small Blues are becoming rarer, too.

Silver-studded Blue

Scientific name: *Plebejus argus*
Wingspan: 29-31 mm
Habitat: Heathland, sand dunes,
limestone grassland
Family: Blues

This small blue butterfly is quite rare
and can only be found in small colonies
in England and Wales. The males have
silvery-blue wings with a black border. Females
have brown upper wings with a row of red spots.
They flutter low over heather.

Common Blue

Scientific name: *Polyommatus icarus*
Wingspan: 29–36 mm
Habitat: Grassland, meadow, woodland, coasts
Family: Blues

Common Blue butterflies can be seen feeding on flowers in a variety of grassy habitats. The upper side of their wings is blue, but the underside is grey-brown with orange markings and white-ringed black spots. Males have very blue upper wings, while females have a dusting of blue, surrounded by brown. Common Blue caterpillars are pale green with yellow stripes.

Holly Blue

Scientific name: *Celastrina argiolus*
Wingspan: 35 mm
Habitat: Gardens, parks, woodland
Family: Blues

Look for Holly Blues near holly bushes in spring and near ivy in summer.

In early spring, the Holly Blue is one of the first blue butterflies to appear. Its blue upper wings are edged with black and it looks very similar to the Common Blue. However, its pale undersides have black spots, which the Common Blue doesn't have. Holly Blues also like to fly high around bushes and trees, whereas the Common Blue stays close to the ground.

Chalk Hill Blue

Scientific name: *Polyommatus coridon*
Wingspan: 38 mm
Habitat: Chalk and limestone grassland
Family: Blues

Male butterflies can be seen feeding on animal dung.

Chalk Hill Blues can be found in the chalk hills of southern England. Males have very light blue wings with a black-and-white border. Females are brown with small orange spots. In August, hundreds of Chalk Hill Blues can be seen flying together.

Brown Argus

Scientific name: *Aricia agestis*
Wingspan: 29 mm
Habitat: Grassland, coasts, woodland, heathland
Family: Blues

The Northern
Brown Argus
looks very similar
but is found only in
northern England
and Scotland

These butterflies are brown
with bright orange spots on their
wing edges. They fly low to the ground
and look very similar to Common Blue females.
Although the Brown Argus is a member of the
Blues family, it actually has no blue on it!

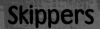

Silver-spotted Skipper

Scientific name: Hesperia comma
Wingspan: 30-36 mm
Habitat: Chalk grassland
Family: Skippers

As its name suggests,
this butterfly has silver spots on the
underside of its hindwings. Its upper wings are
orange with pale orange spots. It is quite rare and can
only be found on the chalk downs of southern England.

Grizzled Skipper

Scientific name: *Pyrgus malvae*
Wingspan: 27 mm
Habitat: Woodland, grassland, heathland, urban habitats
Family: Skippers

This small black-and-white butterfly can be found in England and Wales, but it is becoming more rare. It is recognisable by its checkerboard pattern on its wings. Look out for it flying low to the ground or feeding on yellow flowers, like bird's-foot-trefoil.

Dingy Skipper

Scientific name: Erynnis tages
Wingspan: 29 mm
Habitat: Grassland, heathland, urban habitats, coasts
Family: Skippers

When it is sunny, the Dingy Skipper likes to bask in the sunlight with wings open.

This butterfly is often mistaken for a moth because of its light-brown colouring. They keep low to the ground, flitting from flower to flower. Dingy Skippers are difficult to spot because their colouring means they are well camouflaged. They are easily confused with Grizzled Skippers.

Large Skipper

Scientific name: *Ochlodes sylvanus*
Wingspan: 33-35 mm
Habitat: Grassland habitats
Family: Skippers

Look out for Large Skippers from the end of May through to August.

This common butterfly can often be found feeding on bramble. Males have a black line on their forewing. Their undersides have faint orange spots. The antennae are pointed and hooked. Look for Large Skippers in hedgerows and churchyards where they bask in the sunlight.

Essex Skippers look like Small Skippers, except that they have black tips at the end of their antennae.

Small Skipper

Scientific name: *Thymelicus sylvestris*
Wingspan: 30 mm
Habitat: Grassland, fields
Family: Skippers

This bright orange butterfly can be seen all through summer. Darting from grass stems to flowers, it is hard to see until it settles on a flower to feed. It holds its wings half open, which is a position common to all skipper butterflies. Small Skippers have orange wings with black edging. Males have a thin black line that runs through the centre of the forewing.

Look out for White-letter Hairstreaks resting on bramble.

White-letter Hairstreak

Scientific name: *Satyrium w-album*
Wingspan: 36 mm
Habitat: Woodland, hedgerows
Family: Hairstreaks

The White-letter Hairstreak is dark brown and has 'W'-shaped streaks of white on its under wings. It also has a patch of orange on its under wings and two tails. This butterfly is hard to spot, because it lives in the tops of elm trees. Elm trees were lost to disease in the 1970s and therefore White-letter Hairstreaks have also become rarer.

Black Hairstreak

Scientific name: *Satyrium pruni*
Wingspan: 37 mm
Habitat: Woodland
Family: Hairstreaks

Look for this butterfly in June and July

Black Hairstreaks are not only very rare,
but are also hard to spot. They like to stay
hidden in thickets of blackthorn. Black Hairstreaks
look similar to White-letter Hairstreaks but the white
streaks aren't in a 'W' shape. Black Hairstreaks' underwings
also have larger patches of orange with black spots.

Green Hairstreak

Scientific name: *Callophrys rubi*
Wingspan: 33 mm
Habitat: Chalk and limestone grassland, moorland, woodland, heathland
Family: Hairstreaks

Look out for these metallic green butterflies on bright-yellow gorse flowers.

The Green Hairstreak is the only green butterfly in Britain. However, it is only green on the underside of its wings; the uppersides are brown. Although it is fairly rare, it can still be seen across the whole of the UK.

Purple Hairstreak

Scientific name: *Favonius quercus*
Wingspan: 37–39 mm
Habitat: Woodland, hedgerows
Family: Hairstreaks

This purple butterfly is hard to spot because it lives in the tops of oak trees. Look for it in the early evening when it might come further down to feed. The male has shiny purple wings edged with black, while the female has purple patches at the top, with dark brown hindwings. Both have a little tail. Their undersides are silvery-grey with an orange eyespot.

Brown Hairstreak

Scientific name: *Thecla betulae*
Wingspan: 38-40 mm
Habitat: Woodland, hedgerows
Family: Hairstreaks

Look for Brown Hairstreaks in ash or blackthorn trees. It also likes bramble bushes.

Female Brown Hairstreaks have large orange patches on their upperwings and pointed hindwings. Both males and females have the white 'hairstreak', as well as orange patches on underwings. However, Brown Hairstreaks are extremely hard to spot as they hide in the tops of trees or in hedgerows. They are also becoming rarer because hedgerows are being cut every year which removes eggs.

Fritillaries

Glanville Fritillary

Scientific name: *Melitaea cinxia*
Wingspan: 41–47 mm
Habitat: Coastal grassland
Family: Fritillaries

This butterfly is named after Lady Eleanor Glanville, who first found this butterfly in the 1690s.

This rare butterfly is now found only on the coasts of the Isle of Wight and the Channel Islands. Its orange-and-black chequered upper wings are quite distinctive. The undersides have bands of orange and white. Look for them feeding on birds–foot trefoil or thrift. They are noticeable by their flight, which has rapid wing beats and then a graceful glide.

High Brown Fritillary

Scientific name: *Argynnis adippe*
Wingspan: 60–67mm
Habitat: Woodland clearings, bracken habitats
Family: Fritillaries

This is one of Britain's most endangered butterflies, which has declined in numbers by over 90 per cent since the 1970s. They are large butterflies with orange-and-black wings. It is very hard to tell High Brown Fritillaries from Dark Green Fritillaries. However, High Brown Fritillaries have orange ringed 'pearls' on the underside of their hindwings, which Dark Green Fritillaries don't have.

49

Dark Green Fritillary

Scientific name: *Argynnis aglaja*
Wingspan: 63-69 mm
Habitat: Grassland, coasts, woodland, bracken habitats
Family: Fritillaries

Look for these butterflies in early morning or early evening sunshine.

Very similar to the rare High Brown Fritillary, this more common fritillary is large with orange-and-black markings. It is seen most often in western England, in Scotland and along the coast of Wales. Dark Green Fritillaries like to feed on thistles and bramble.

Silver-washed Fritillary

Scientific name: *Argynnis paphia*
Wingspan: 72-76 mm
Habitat: Woodland
Family: Fritillaries

Look for these butterflies in woodland glades

This is a large, fast-flying
butterfly. It is different from
other fritillaries because it has pointed
wings and silver streaks on the undersides.
Males have four black stripes across the forewings.
They like to feed on bramble.

Marsh Fritillary

Scientific name: *Euphydryas aurinia*
Wingspan: 42–48 mm
Habitat: Damp grassland, chalk and
limestone grassland
Family: Fritillaries

The Marsh Fritillary is
a brightly coloured butterfly
with bands of black and orange, dotted
with paler orange spots. It is the most colourful
of the fritillary family. This rare butterfly can now only be
found in a few spots across Britain, including places in Wales,
south-west England and Scotland.

Pearl-bordered Fritillary

Scientific name: *Boloria euphrosyne*
Wingspan: 44–47 mm
Habitat: Woodland clearings, bracken habitats
Family: Fritillaries

Easily confused with the Small Pearl-bordered Fritillary, the Pearl-bordered Fritillary has two large silver pearls and seven outer pearls on the underside hindwing. These outer pearls are bordered with red chevrons. (The Small Pearl-bordered Fritillary has black chevrons.) This is one the earliest Fritillaries to emerge and can be seen from April. Look for them on bracken-covered hillsides.

Small Pearl-bordered Fritillary

Scientific name: *Boloria selene*
Wingspan: 41-44 mm
Habitat: Woodland, moorland, grassland and bracken habitats
Family: Fritilliaries

Despite its name,
the Small Pearl-bordered
Fritillary is actually of a similar size to
the Pearl-bordered Fritillary. The main difference
between these two butterflies is the black chevrons on
their underwings (the Pearl-bordered has red). This butterfly
is also more common, particularly in Wales and Scotland. It flies
close to the ground and feeds on bramble and other flowers.

Duke of Burgundy

Scientific name: *Hamearis lucina*
Wingspan: 29-32 mm
Habitat: Chalk and limestone grassland, woodland
Family: Metalmarks

Look for this butterfly in May and June.

This small butterfly is becoming increasingly rare. Its upperwings are dark brown with bright orange spots and there are large white spots on its hindwings. Although once classified as a fritillary, the Duke of Burgundy is actually the only British member of a subfamily called the metalmarks.

Small Copper

Scientific name: *Lycaena phlaeas*
Wingspan: 32–35 mm
Habitat: Grassland, woodland
Family: Coppers

Look for Small Copper butterflies feeding on ragwort or thistles.

This fast-flying butterfly can be seen from April right through until September. Its bright copper-coloured upper wings are dotted with black spots. Its undersides are a lighter brown. Small Coppers can usually be found in ones or twos.

Swallowtail

Scientific name: *Papilio machaon*
Wingspan: 80-90 mm
Habitat: Reedbeds, marshland
Family: Swallowtails

Swallowtail butterflies like to feed on ragged-robin flowers.

These distinctive, large butterflies can only be found in the Norfolk Broads. They are one of the rarest, as well as largest, British butterflies. They have pale yellow wings with striking black veins and a red spot. The hindwings each have a distinctive pointed tail.

How to protect butterflies

Butterflies are threatened by habitat loss, climate change and pollution. Habitats are changed, because the land becomes used for a different purpose, such as agriculture or building. Pollution and climate change affect the plants and flowers that butterflies and caterpillars rely on for food and shelter.

Flower gardens

You can help to protect butterflies by planting nectar-rich flowers in your garden. Butterflies use these plants to get nectar, so try to ensure that you have flowers in bloom throughout spring, summer and autumn.

If you have a big garden, why not leave an area to grow wild? This will encourage many types of insects, not just butterflies. Areas of long grass and features such as trees and hedgerows provide food for caterpillars, and shelter over the winter months. Leave a nettle patch for butterflies such as Red Admiral, Comma and Small Tortoiseshell. In winter, don't cut back shrubs and plants until the following spring. For the best flowers for your garden, go to:

http://butterfly-conservation.org/files/100-best-butterfly-nectar-plants.pdf

You will need:
• A large plant pot
• Soil
• Seeds or flowering plants

How to plant flowerpots

You don't have to buy new pots or containers for your plants. Reuse containers such as washing-up bowls, plastic toy crates or even old wellington boots. Plants will spread as they grow so the bigger the container, the better.

1 Make sure your container has holes at the bottom to let any excess water drain out. You might need to ask an adult to help you put holes in them.

3 Scatter your seeds on top and gently cover with more soil.

2 Fill the container with soil to about three-quarters of the way up.

4 Alternatively, if you have bought plants, dig holes and place the plants in the holes. Firm the plant in.

5 Water your container. Remember to water the plants as soon as the soil looks dry. This is usually every 2 or 3 days, but on hot summer days, this will be every day.

6 Place your pot in a sunny place and your plants will soon start to flower.

In garden centres, look for plants marked pollinator-friendly.

Further information

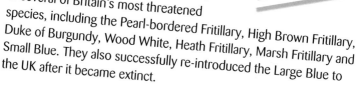

Butterfly Conservation

Butterfly Conservation is a charity supported by Sir David Attenborough as President. It has raised awareness of the drastic decline in butterflies and moths and, through conservation work, has begun to reverse the decline of several of Britain's most threatened species, including the Pearl-bordered Fritillary, High Brown Fritillary, Duke of Burgundy, Wood White, Heath Fritillary, Marsh Fritillary and Small Blue. They also successfully re-introduced the Large Blue to the UK after it became extinct.

Butterfly Conservation run three of the world's largest butterfly and moth recording schemes, including the 'Big Butterfly Count' in July and August. This event helps to record butterfly species in the UK so that steps can be taken to protect them if their numbers are found to be declining. Find out how you can take part at:
www.bigbutterflycount.org

Find out how to identify butterflies with their A-Z guide:
www.butterfly-conservation.org/679/a-z-of-butterflies.html

The websites also give lots of information on how you can help from gardening tips to joining and getting involved with your local branch. You can also download some fantastic children's resources at:
www.munchingcaterpillars.org

Useful websites and places to visit

The National Trust takes care of many different habitats and nature reserves as well as historic houses and gardens. Find out about the top ten butterfly walks at:
www.nationaltrust.org.uk/lists/butterfly-walks

Top tips for butterfly spotting:
www.nationaltrust.org.uk/features/top-tips-for-butterfly-spotting

The Wildlife Trusts website recommends places across Britain that are good for spotting all types of insects, including butterflies.
www.wildlifetrusts.org/woodlandbutterflies

The Woodland Trust's Nature Detective's website includes activity sheets and ideas such as how to make a butterfly feeder.
www.woodlandtrust.org.uk/naturedetectives/activities/beautiful-butterflies/

The Natural History Museum website has lots of information about butterflies. For tips on how to attract butterflies to your garden, go to:
http://www.nhm.ac.uk/discover/how-to-attract-butterflies.html

Find out about some record-breaking butterflies:
www.nhm.ac.uk/discover/record-breaking-butterflies.html

Or read about the world's oldest butterflies:
www.nhm.ac.uk/discover/adventures-worlds-oldest-butterflies.html

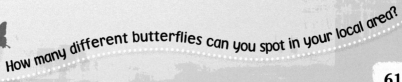

How many different butterflies can you spot in your local area?

Glossary

abdomen the back part of an insect, joined to the thorax

antennae an insect's feelers, its sense organ for smell and touch

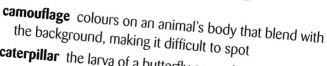

camouflage colours on an animal's body that blend with the background, making it difficult to spot

caterpillar the larva of a butterfly or moth

chrysalis (*plural: chrysalises*) the stage where a caterpillar forms a hard shell and changes into a butterfly

climate change the change of weather patterns around the world, caused by pollution

colony a group of insects that live together

environment all the things that surround animals and plants in the natural world, such as air, soil and water

extinct no longer existing

eyespot a spot that looks like an eye

food chain the link between plants and animals showing who eats who

forewing the front, or forward, wing of an insect

habitat a place where a plant or an animal lives in the wild

hibernate to spend the winter sleeping or resting

hindwing the back, or backward, wing of an insect

larvae the young of insects that have hatched from their egg